YOU'RE A GOOD FRIEND,
CAPYBARA

YOU'RE A GOOD FRIEND, CAPYBARA

CHRONICLE BOOKS
San Francisco

HELLO!
I'M A CAPYBARA!
I KNOW A THING
OR TWO ABOUT BEING
A GOOD FRIEND.

Because we capybaras make friends with creatures of all shapes and sizes,

we know all the ways to make a friendship blossom, and what it means to be a good friend.

GOOD FRIENDS
ARE THE ONES WHO
LIFT YOU UP
AND MAKE YOU
FEEL TALL.

THEY WATCH
YOUR BACK
WHEN THE GOING
GETS TOUGH.

AND THEY'LL
ALWAYS LEND AN
EAR WHEN YOU
NEED TO VENT.

"Guess who ate MY lunch again today!"

Whether you prefer big parties

or plenty of alone time . . .

A good friend will follow you anywhere

and knows when to give you space.

A GOOD FRIEND
WILL ALWAYS MAKE
SURE YOU BOTH
SELFIE FROM YOUR
BEST SIDES.

Friends not only have your back, they also make you feel like you have wings.

"You wanna talk to my friend? You gotta go through me!"

Good friends come running when you call

and they're always happy to see you.

EVEN WHEN

YOUR FRIENDS ARE

FAR AWAY . . .

. . . IT'S IMPORTANT
TO MAKE THEM
FEEL THAT YOU'RE
ALWAYS CLOSE BY.

"I WAS JUST
THINKING ABOUT YOU!
HOW ARE YOU?"

GOOD FRIENDS

REMEMBER YOUR

FAVORITE

KARAOKE SONGS.

"Don't stop . . . BELIEVIN'!"

Time with friends may involve comfortable silences

or fierce debates.

Friends are up for a bit of mischief when you want it

and for keeping on the straight and narrow when you need it.

Sometimes your best friend comes from the same herd

and you grow up side by side.

Sometimes you find friends in unexpected places

and your forever friends become your new herd.

FRIENDSHIPS

COME IN ALL SIZES:

BIG . . .

. . . AND
SMALL.

YOU NEVER KNOW,
MAYBE YOUR CLOSEST
FRIENDS WILL TURN
OUT TO BE YOUR
HOUSEPLANTS!

"All the best gardeners say talking to your plants helps them grow."

FRIENDS DON'T
MIND SHARING
THEIR FOOD—EVEN
WHEN IT'S THEIR
FAVORITE DESSERT.

FRIENDS MAY
SHOW THEY CARE BY
PREPARING A
HOME-COOKED MEAL.

AND THEY WILL
ALWAYS COMPLIMENT
YOUR COOKING, EVEN
IF IT'S ONLY SALAD.

"Kale! My favorite! How did you know?"

You can count on friends to hold your place in line

or come to your dance recital.

GOOD FRIENDS
WILL LAUGH AT
YOUR JOKES, EVEN
IF YOU'VE TOLD
THEM BEFORE.

"Why are capybaras always smiling? Because they're cappy!"

A FRIEND IS SOMEONE
YOU TURN TO ON DAYS
WHEN YOU HAVE
TROUBLE COMING OUT
OF YOUR SHELL . . .

. . . OR ON DAYS
WHEN YOU JUST NEED
SOMEONE TO APPRECIATE
YOUR NEWEST FASHION
STATEMENT.

EVERYTHING IS MORE FUN WITH FRIENDS.

Going for a swim

Taking a nap

Long walks together

Spa days

Good friends offer the encouragement you need to work out

or the excuse you want to stay home and eat snacks.

EVEN BIRD-WATCHING
IS BETTER WITH FRIENDS,
ESPECIALLY WHEN YOUR
FRIENDS ARE BIRDS.

Friends may not always see eye to eye on everything, and even best friends get into fights.

But afterward, it's important to extend an olive branch. "I'm sorry" is as meaningful as "I love you."

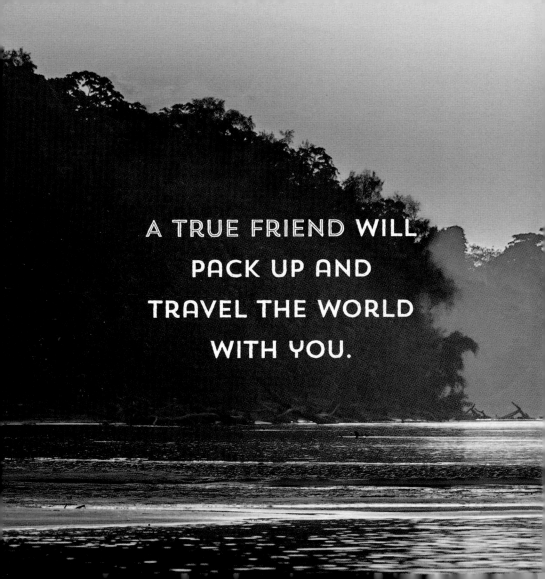

WHEN LIFE MAKES
IT HARD TO PICK
YOURSELF UP . . .

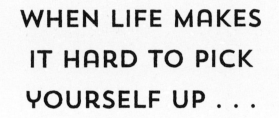

. . . A GOOD
FRIEND WILL BE
THERE TO HELP
CARRY YOU
THROUGH IT ALL.

SO WHEN YOU NEED
SOMEONE TO WALK OFF
INTO THE SUNSET WITH,
JUST REMEMBER:

BEST FRIENDS ARE FOREVER.

"Wanna get fries on the way home?"

A FEW CAPY FAQS:

What are capybaras?

Native to South America, capybaras are the largest rodents in the world (sometimes up to 4 feet, or 1.2 metres, long). Although they look a bit like giant hamsters, their closest relatives are actually guinea pigs!

Capybaras have slightly webbed feet, making them excellent swimmers, and in the wild, they tend to live near lakes, marshes, or rivers. They can also hold their breath underwater for up to five minutes, which can help them escape predators. They can even sleep in the water, since their eyes, ears, and nose are set high on their heads and can stay above the surface while they snooze.

Capybaras are herbivores and use their large, very sharp front teeth to chew through up to 8 pounds (3.6 kilogrammes) of grasses and other plants per day. They also eat their own poop, for health benefits. (Yes, really.)

Are they really friends with other animals?

Capybaras, unlike some other rodents, are very social animals. They tend to live in herds of 10 or more fellow capybaras in the wild and in certain seasons can be found in groups of up to 40 at a time. They share a symbiotic relationship with many types of birds, who use them as a rest stop in exchange for keeping insects away. Capybaras have a very calm manner around other animals and humans—though like most prey animals, they're wary of predators in the wild and can move very quickly when threatened. Capybaras raised in captivity have been observed to bond with a wide variety of other animals, including cats, monkeys, dogs, turtles, and more—some of which can be seen in this book. This has led to capybaras having a reputation for being chill, friendly animals.

What about the alligators?

Caimans, included earlier in these pages, are cousins of alligators and indeed a natural predator of the capybara. However, caimans and capybaras have also been observed sitting peacefully together in the wild. It's not entirely certain why this happens. Maybe it's because a herd of fully grown capybaras makes a difficult midday snack and not worth the effort, or because capybaras are not the brightest of prey, or possibly because, some afternoons, it's just nice to gather together and commiserate over your shared fear of jaguars.

Can I have a capybara as a pet?

Despite their relation to guinea pigs, capybaras are not domesticated—they are wild animals and should not be kept as pets. Some capybaras live in rescue sanctuaries, farms, or zoos and are unable to return safely to the wild. But similar to other wild animals, capybaras require a lot of specialized care and maintenance. If you wish to fantasize about a capybara friend, we recommend returning to the beginning of this book (which will conveniently never bite, eat, or poop) to reread and enjoy—or visit capybaras at your nearest local zoo.

Thank you for being a friend to capys everywhere!

Library of Congress Cataloging-in-Publication Data

Names: Chronicle Books (Firm)
Title: You're a good friend, capybara / Chronicle Books.
Description: San Francisco : Chronicle Books, 2021.
Identifiers: LCCN 2021007821 | ISBN 9781797210575 (hardcover)
Subjects: LCSH: Capybara. | LCGFT: Illustrated works.
Classification: LCC QL737.R662 Y68 2021 | DDC 599.35/9--dc23
LC record available at https://lccn.loc.gov/2021007821

Manufactured in China.

MIX
Paper from responsible sources
FSC
www.fsc.org   FSC™ C104723

Design by Kim Di Santo.

10 9 8 7 6 5 4 3 2 1

Photos courtesy of:

Front cover and 74: © Bruno Conjeaud.

Back cover, 6, 18, 28, 32, 33, 39, 47, 51, 55, and 65: © Janice Wolf of Rocky Ridge Refuge.

Back cover, 31: Haiwei Hu/500px Prime via Getty Images ; **Back cover, 59:** Hannari_eli/Shutterstock.com; **Back cover, 62:** shot by supervliegzus/Moment via Getty Images; **Back cover, 63:** Shin Okamoto/Shutterstock.com

Icons: Mila_Endo/Shutterstock.com and Kozyreva Elena/Shutterstock.com; **2:** GTW/Shutterstock.com; **4:** Kathy Matsunami/Shutterstock.com; **7:** Y_Hirosan/Shutterstock.com; **9:** CoralCapy/Shutterstock.com; **10:** Edwin Butter/Shutterstock.com; **13:** Luciana Biazzi/Shutterstock.com; **14:** jaboticaba images/Shutterstock.com; **15:** Maarten Zeehandelaar/Shutterstock.com; **16–17, 24–25:** Vadim Petrakov/Shutterstock.com; **20:** Julio duarte/Shutterstock.com; **21:** Guilherme Sementili/Shutterstock.com; **22–23:** slowmotiongli/Shutterstock.com; **27:** boss19662008/Shutterstock.com; **34:** Ilya D. Gridnev/Shutterstock.com; **35:** IamTK/Shutterstock.com; **36:** Steve Meese/Shutterstock.com; **37:** Kletr/Shutterstock.com; **38:** Brad Fish/Shutterstock.com; **41:** meunierd/Shutterstock.com; **42:** Vinicius Bacarin/Shutterstock.com; **45:** Pablo Rodriguez Merkel/Shutterstock.com; **48:** Japan's Fireworks/Shutterstock.com; **52:** sergiodbj/Shutterstock.com; **53:** ROBERTA BLONKOWSKI/Shutterstock.com; **56:** CoralCapy/Shutterstock.com; **60:** jeurboy/Shutterstock.com; **61:** JuLauletta/Shutterstock.com; **64:** foto_monteiro/Shutterstock.com; **67:** Kristina Gain/Shutterstock.com; **68:** M.Antonello Photography/Shutterstock.com; **69:** LouieLea/Shutterstock.com; **70–71:** RPBaiao/Shutterstock.com; **73:** Christian Musat/Shutterstock.com; **76–78:** Ondrej Prosicky/Shutterstock.com; **80:** Tokunaga226/Shutterstock.com

Chronicle Books LLC
680 Second Street
San Francisco, California 94107

www.chroniclebooks.com

Goodbye, friend!